START PLAYING KEYBOARD
OMNIBUS EDITION:BOOKS 1 & 2
by Peter Lavender

Amsco Publications
New York/London/Sydney

Order No. AM 67588
International Standard Book Number: 0.8256.1187.3

Exclusive Distributors:

Music Sales Corporation
257 Park Avenue South, New York, NY 10010, USA
Music Sales Limited
8/9 Frith Street, London W1V 5TZ England
Music Sales Pty. Limited
120 Rothschild Street, Rosebery, Sydney, NSW 2018, Australia

Printed in the United States of America by
Vicks Lithograph and Printing Corporation

Part 1

Part 2

SFX—SOUNDS 'N' EFFECTS
PART 1

About This Book

Welcome to SFX music.

When you play music the SFX way, you become a performing musician almost from the word 'go'. That's because SFX music is easy to read . . . quick to learn . . . and fun to play. What's more, there are SFX music books to suit all tastes and for all occasions.

Before you start, here are a few tips which you will find useful:

Always use the right sound, the right rhythm and the right tempo. The choice of these settings depends on the particular tune you are playing. For instance, you wouldn't put a 'brassy' sound suitable for a march with a gentle waltz. So whenever you play a song, always decide on registrations which fit. A change in the tempo of the rhythm changes the character of a piece of music. Always keep the tempo down to a reasonable speed until you've mastered the melody. And never play a background effect so loud that it over-rides the melody.

Follow the suggested registrations in this book along with rhythm and tempo settings. They are a starting guide while you learn and enjoy playing SFX music.

Finally, get to know all the Sounds 'n' Effects on your keyboard. Explore these exciting features from the start. Vary the sounds and rhythms every time you play the tunes through.

Have Fun.

All keyboard instruments have the same layout of black and white keys.

The black keys are arranged in alternate groups of 2 and 3 notes:

A melody played on the keyboard is a sequence of musical tones. Each of these tones can be written as **music notes** on and around the **staff**.

The staff (or "Stave" as it is sometimes called) has 5 **lines** and 4 **spaces**.

A treble clef sign is placed at the beginning of the first staff in all SFX music to indicate that the notes are for right hand melody playing:

Each line and space has a letter name by which music notes appearing in the staff are identified.

To help you to play your favourite tunes straight away, all music notes in SFX songbooks show their letter names.

This makes SFX music as simple as

In music the first seven letters of the alphabet are used, and this is how they appear in SFX notes:

In SFX songbooks, most of the tunes use notes from **middle C** upwards on your keyboard.

Middle C is in the centre area of the keyboard, immediately left of **two black keys:**

The middle C note is written just below the staff. A short line (called a Ledger Line) cuts through the note head.

The first 5 right hand melody notes, starting from Middle C, go **up** the keyboard and **up** the staff.

Position your right hand just above the keyboard, with a slight downward curve of the fingers. Starting with the thumb (finger number 1), play Middle C. Release the key then play the next note D (finger 2), release, and on to E (finger 3), F (finger 4), and lastly G with the 5th finger.

Repeat this several times to get the feel of the keys. Try to keep your eyes on each note of music in the staff as you play its key.

Now reverse the sequence. Starting on G (5th finger), play each note in turn, back down to Middle C.

Finally, play all five notes **up** and then back **down** again. Important playing 'pointers': keep your eyes on the music, don't let your hand sag at the wrist, and play all the notes evenly with an equal sounding time for each tone.

Music notes. There are three main types of music notes, each having a *time value* that is counted in regular **beats**:

The WHOLE NOTE = ○ = 4 BEATS

The HALF NOTE = = 2 BEATS

The QUARTER NOTE = = 1 BEAT

Bar lines are vertical lines that appear throughout the staff. The distance between two bar lines is called a **measure**. Each measure contains a fixed number of beats depending on the type of music. A double bar line is always placed at the end of a piece of music:

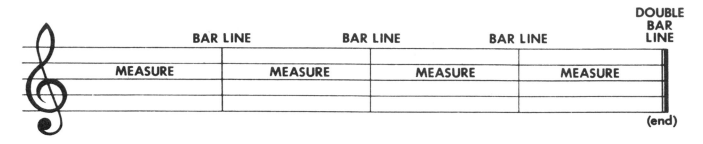

The time signature always appears at the beginning of the music. It tells you the number of beats in each measure, and the type of note that will represent one beat.

The top number in the time signature shows the amount of beats in each measure.

The bottom number indicates the type of note that will have *one* beat. In this "Four-four" time signature, the lower 4 represents the *Quarter Note.*

All other types of notes that occur in the "Four-four" time will be governed by the Quarter Note time value of one beat:

Some well known tunes can now be played on your keyboard using the notes learned so far.

Play the first five melodies with your *right hand only*, using the fingering marked alongside the notes. Take care to give each note its correct time value — the beat count is given in the first few measures.

When you have become familiar with playing these tunes with the right hand, the *left hand accompaniment* can be added.

The following letters appear above the music staff:

These are the names of **chords**. A chord is several musical tones sounding together, providing accompaniment to the melody. By simply playing the appropriate key in the chord section of the keyboard with your left hand, the instrument will automatically produce this accompaniment.

Your Owner's Manual will fully explain the automatic chord function and other similar features programmed into the keyboard.

Au Clair De La Lune

Traditional

Largo

Dvorak

Suggested Registration:
PIANO
or
STRINGS

Merrily We Roll Along

Traditional

Suggested Registration:
PIANO
or
TRUMPET

Mer - ri - ly We Roll A - long, roll a - long, roll a - long,

Mer - ri - ly We Roll A - long, o'er the deep blue sea.

The next song introduces the "7th" type of chord:

When using automatic chord accompaniment, your Owner's Manual will explain the simple two-finger left hand key position that produces 7th chords.

If the 7th chord is not programmed into your keyboard, disregard the figure 7 appearing outside the chord symbol box — the basic chord will provide adequate accompaniment to the melody.

Lightly Row

Traditional

12

Jingle Bells

Traditional

When you have played these tunes through with chord accompaniment, try adding **rhythm.** Your Owner's Manual will explain this feature.

Set the *Tempo* at **medium** speed, with **swing, soft rock,** or similar 'four-to-the-measure' pattern.

Waltz time is often referred to as "three-four time", as can be seen from the popular waltz time signature:

This time signature indicates there are 3 Quarter Notes, each with a beat, in **every** measure:

The Dotted Half Note. When a dot is placed after a note, the *time value* of that note is increased by one-half of its value. The Dotted Half Note therefore has a count of 3 beats:

The Tie is a curved line that links consecutive notes on the same line or in the **same** space of the staff. When a tie appears in the music, play the first note and sustain the sound for the full time value of the tied note sequence:

Barcarolle

from "The Tales Of Hoffman"

Rhythm:	Tempo:
WALTZ	MEDIUM

Suggested Registration:
CLASSICAL ORGAN
or
STRINGS

Pick Up Notes occur when a piece of music starts with one or several notes that do not total a full measure. They are played at their usual time value. In most cases the last measure of music rounds everything off by supplying the missing beat. A double bar line usually follows Pick Up Notes.

The words NO CHORD sometimes appear above Pick Up Notes indicating they are best played without accompaniment. This is when the RHYTHM "SYNCHRO" feature on your keyboard can be used most effectively. The Pick Up Notes are played without rhythm, and the "Synchro" feature will start the rhythm immediately you add the chord accompaniment.

The old jazz favourite "When The Saints Go Marching In" begins with three Quarter Notes in 4/4 time signature.

When The Saints Go Marching In

The next songs introduce three new notes in the music staff — A, B and C:

By using the fingering marked alongside music notes in these songs, your right hand melody playing will develop a smooth and confident playing style.

Michael Row the Boat Ashore

Traditional

| Suggested Registration:
BRASS
or
PIANO | | Rhythm:
SWING
or
ROCK | Tempo:
MEDIUM |

Mi - chael Row The Boat A - shore, Hal - le -

lu - jah, Mi - chael Row The Boat A -

shore, Hal - le - lu - jah. Bro - ther

lend a help - ing hand, Hal - le - lu - jah, Bro - ther

She Wore A Yellow Ribbon
Traditional

Repeat signs are often used in a song when a part or sometimes all of the melody is to be played through again. They save space and unnecessary turning of pages:

All music appearing between the Repeat Signs is to be replayed.

The word **fine** in the last measure of this song means 'End' — the point to finish playing after the Repeat has been made.

On Top of Old Smokey

Quite often there will only be one Repeat Sign that appears at the end of a section of music. The repeat is then made from the very beginning:

Chopsticks

Double Endings. Sometimes a change in the melody will occur for one or several measures towards the end of a repeat section of music. Double Endings, using 1st and 2nd time brackets above the staff, mark off where a short 'skip' is to be made after the repeat has been played through:

Muss I Denn (Must I Then)

Traditional

Suggested Registration:
PIANO
or
VIBRAPHONE

Rhythm:
SWING
or
SOFT ROCK

Tempo:
MEDIUM

For if you love me as I love

you, Then a mill - ion miles dis - ap - pear.

When I go from your side, I will not be sad and

blue, Don't cry my darl - ing true, Keep my

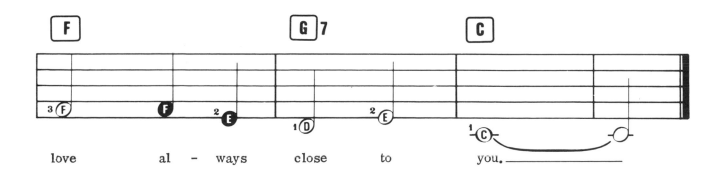

love al - ways close to you.

The "Can Can" has a series of notes running down in the 7th and 8th measures. Try to get a smooth cross-fingering between the notes F and E in the 8th measure.

Can-Can

Offenbach

Suggested Registration: BRASS or VIBRAPHONE	Rhythm: SWING or ROCK	Tempo: MEDIUM FAST

Five new notes continue up the staff, with a ledger line for the last note:

She'll be Coming Around the Mountain

Traditional

Where Have All The Flowers Gone?

Words and Music by Pete Seeger

| Suggested Registration:
FLUTE
or
STRINGS | Rhythm:
BEGUINE/RHUMBA
or
SOFT ROCK | Tempo:
MEDIUM |

This song introduces a new chord:

Love Me Tender

Words and Music by Elvis Presley and Vera Matson

Snow Waltz

Traditional

Suggested Registration: VIBRAPHONE or PIANO	Rhythm: WALTZ	Tempo: MEDIUM FAST

Everyone's Gone to the Moon

Words & Music by Jonathan King

The Eighth Note has a tail:

In pairs, and groups of 4, the tails become *beams*:

The Eighth Note has a time value that is one-half of a Quarter Note. A pair of Eighth Notes therefore equal one Quarter Note:

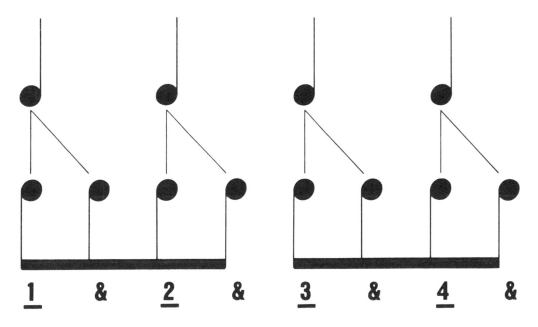

The "&" used in the Eighth Note count is one way to split the Quarter Note beat.

Another method is to tap your foot in time to the beat. Each down-and-up movement of the toe is a pair of Eighth Notes forming 1 beat.

Skip To My Lou

Traditional

Dance Little Bird

Words and Music by Werner Thomas and Terry Rendall

The Dotted Quarter Note.
When a dot appears after the
Quarter Note, its value is
increased by one half:

= 1 beat, + "½ for the dot"
= 1½ **beats.**

**The Dotted Quarter Note is
usually followed by an Eighth
Note to make a full two-beat
phrase:**

New chord: C 7

Silent Night

Traditional

Suggested Registration:
STRINGS
or
FLUTE

Rhythm:
WALTZ

Tempo:
MEDIUM

Rests. All our music so far has been a variety of different sounding notes, with a mixture of note values to give rhythm to the flow of musical sounds.

There are moments in all kinds of music however, when a complete silence is briefly needed. These rests are also handy for the casual fingering or "sound" change!

Rests are musical symbols that are written in the staff, and like music notes, each rest has a time value:

WHOLE REST
(4 Beats)

HALF REST
(2 Beats)

QUARTER REST
(1 Beat)

EIGHTH REST
(½ Beat)

1 2 3 4   1   2   3   4   1   2   3   4   1   &   2   &   3   &   4   &

Gonna Build A Mountain

From The Musical Production "Stop The World I Want To Get Off"

Minor Chords. The next song introduces the *Minor* chords:

When using automatic chord accompaniment, your Keyboard Owner's Manual will explain the simple two-finger key position in the left hand that produces Minor chord accompaniment.

Goodbye

Words and Music by John Lennon and Paul McCartney

Sharps and flats. By the occasional use of the black notes on your keyboard, SFX music now opens up the way for you to play all the great songs in the SFX music books.

This music symbol is the **sharp**:

When it appears just before a note, simply play the *black key* that lies immediately to the *right* of the white key.

This has the effect of **sharp**ening the musical pitch of the written note:

The next song introduces three new chords: Dm E7 A7

I Left My Heart In San Francisco

Words by Douglass Cross
Music by George Cory

39

fog   may chill the   air,   I don't care!   My love waits

there,   in San Fran - cis - co,   A - bove the

blue   and wind - y   sea.   When   I   come

home   to   you, San Fran - cis - co,   your gold - en

sun   will   shine   for   me.

New chords:

Annie's Song

Words and Music by John Denver

This is the music symbol called the **flat**: ♭

A flat placed before a note tells you to play the *black key* lying immediately to the **left** of the *white key*. This time, the musical pitch becomes **flat**tened:

42

New chords:

A Hard Day's Night

Words and Music by John Lennon and Paul McCartney

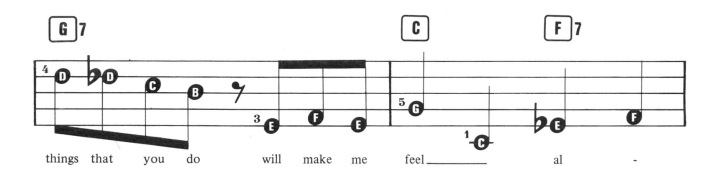

things that you do will make me feel _____ al -

right. When I'm home, Ev - 'ry - thing seems to be

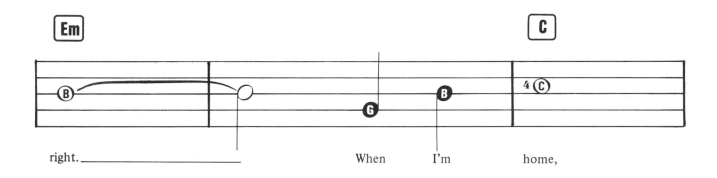

right. _____ When I'm home,

Feel - ing you hold - ing me tight, tight. It's Been A

Sometimes, a tune will contain both sharps and flats:

Melody of Love

Music by H. Engelmann. Words by Tom Glazer.

Suggested Registration: OBOE or PIANO	Rhythm: SWING or SOFT ROCK	Tempo: MEDIUM

The Triplet. This is a group of *three notes* that are all played in the same amount of time as *two notes* of the same value.

The triplet has a small figure 3 placed either above or below the note group:

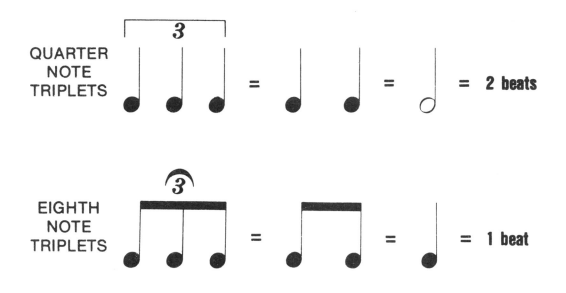

The religious ballad "Amazing Grace" has *Eighth Note Triplets* that contrast effectively with pairs of *Eighth Notes* in other measures:

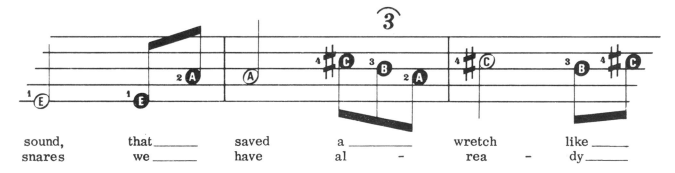

The words **D.S. al Fine** appear at the end of the music. This means return to the **sign:**—

The music is then played through again, and ends at **Fine** in the usual manner.

"Amazing Grace" is an extended arrangement that uses several sharps in the first chorus, followed by a 'lift' in the music pitch for the second chorus. This is known as a **key change**, and flats become a feature of the new key:

Amazing Grace

Traditional

Suggested Registration:
STRINGS
or
TRUMPET

Rhythm:
WALTZ

Tempo:
MEDIUM

now I see._____ 'Twas grace that_____
lead us home._____

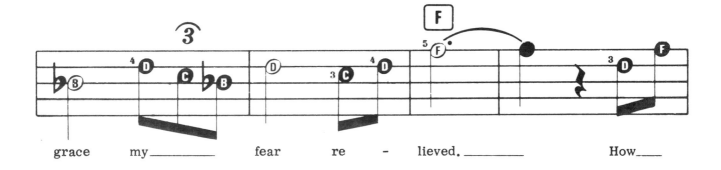

taught my heart to fear, and_____

grace my_____ fear re - lieved._____ How_____

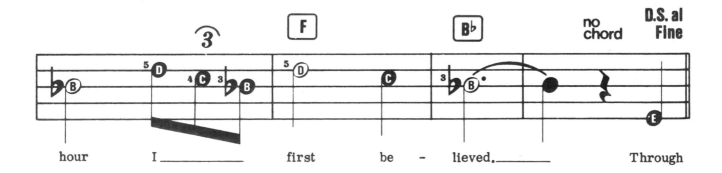

pre - cious_____ did that grace app - ear, The_____

hour I_____ first be - lieved._____ Through

Left Hand Fingered Chords. Although this book has centered around the automatic features on your keyboard that provide such effective accompaniment to SFX songs, there is an interesting alternative in using *Left Hand Fingered Chords.* Accompaniment for the melody is made with the left hand playing groups of three or four notes — the chords — in the lower section of your keyboard.

If your keyboard can be switched from 'Automatic' to 'Fingered' accompaniment mode, it is recommended that you learn this type of chord playing.

The step-by-step learning and use of fingered chords will open up exciting new ventures into the world of creative music making through SFX publications.

MASTER CHORD CHART

SFX–SOUNDS 'N' EFFECTS
PART 2

Part 1 of the SFX method showed you how to play popular tunes on your keyboard in a quick and easy way by using the unique SFX letter-note music system and the 'one finger' automatic chord feature.

Part 2 will show you
(1) how to play the professional style 'fingered' chords in your left hand
(2) how to improve and perfect your sight reading and overall playing technique
(3) an easy transition from SFX letter-note music to standard music notation. This is a major step forward in music making that will enable you to play tunes on your keyboard from the immensely popular fake books, and the single note (vocal) lines in everyday sheet music.

Well known melodies have been chosen to help you learn more about music and modern keyboard techniques. Keep exploring all the Sounds 'n' Effects – instrument voices, rhythms, fill ins, tempos, and the add-on effects like vibrato, sustain, reverb, arpeggios, bass accompaniments, sound modulations etc.

Listen to, and play, *all* kinds of music. There are lots of good sounds around!

PL

'Fingered' Chords. The one-finger automatic chord feature on your keyboard enables you to play tunes in a quick and easy way, with a variety of accompaniment effects.

To get the maximum enjoyment and musical benefit from your keyboard, it is recommended you also learn to play all the tunes in the SFX method using 'Fingered' chords. Your Owner's Manual will explain how this feature operates on the keyboard.

The first 15 tunes in SFX-Tutor Part 1 use the chords of C, G, G7 and F; finger positions for left hand are illustrated below. Practise these four basic chords, keeping your wrist just above keyboard level and fingers slightly curved onto each of the notes to be played. The fingering numbers are a general guide only, as you may find it easier to use different fingering between more rapid chord changes later.

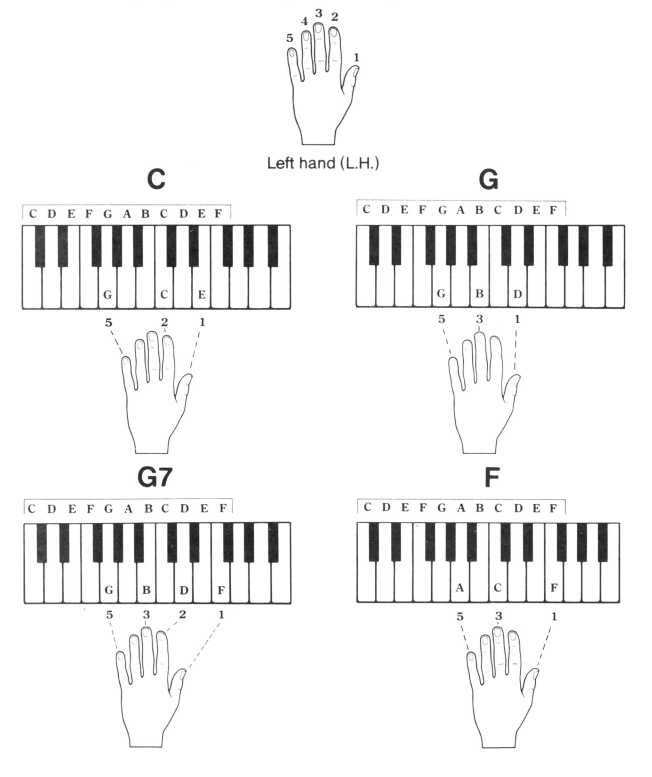

The following 'fingered' chords can be used to play the remaining tunes in
SFX-Tutor Part 1.

The well known tunes you are about to play will introduce new 'fingered' chords. Learn
them, and you will soon be familiar with their sequences in popular music.

A useful 3-point practice routine: (1) play the melody on its own with the right hand,
(2) repeat several times using the 'one finger' automatic chord accompaniment, and
finally (3) play the song using 'fingered' chords.

By following this routine, and using the variety of Sounds 'n' Effects on your keyboard,
you will become a competent and creative player.

52

The Quarter Note Triplet:

Quarter note triplets are very popular in slow ballads. This song from West Side Story makes effective use of these 'laid back' phrases.

New chords: Cm   Gm

Somewhere
(From the Broadway Musical "West Side Story")

Music by Leonard Bernstein Lyrics by Stephen Sondheim

The next song has two separate Repeat sections. The latter (Repeat) has a combined 1st and 2nd time bracket, with the 3rd time bracket providing the final chord and melody note.

Feelings (Dime)

English Words & Music by Morris Albert
Spanish Lyric by Thomas Fundora

The Sixteenth Note has two tails:

In pairs, and groups of four, the tails become parallel beams:

The Sixteenth Note has a time value that is one-half of an Eighth Note. A pair of Sixteenth Notes therefore equals one Eighth Note:

The following three measures each show how notes of similar value appear in $\frac{4}{4}$ time. Play the sequence through at a steady tempo, following the counting guide below each note.

Sixteenth notes are frequently beamed to dotted eighth notes. This follows the rule that a dot after a note increases its value by one-half:

It is the little extra time value, and resulting natural stress on each dotted note, that gives the bouncy 'lilt' to many songs like the ever popular Beatles hit "Yellow Submarine".

Yellow Submarine
Words and Music by John Lennon and Paul McCartney

Yel - low Sub - ma - rine.　In　the　town＿＿＿＿　where　I　was
　　　　　　　　　　　　　　　　　　　　sailed＿＿＿＿　up　to　the

born,　　Lived　a　man＿＿＿＿＿　who　sailed　the
sun,　　Till　we　found＿＿＿＿＿　the　sea　of

sea.　　　And　he　told＿＿＿＿＿＿＿　us　of　his
green.　　And　we　lived＿＿＿＿＿＿＿　be - neath　the

life,　　In　the　land＿＿＿＿＿＿＿　of　sub - ma -
waves,　In　our　Yel - low　　Sub - ma -

rines.　　So　we　rine.

Toreador Song has both eighth note, and dotted eighth note/sixteenth note patterns. Played correctly, these contrasting rhythmic phrases add extra spirit to this famous tune.

Toreador Song (from "Carmen")

By Georges Bizet

Paul Simon's "59th St. Bridge Song" also features eighth note and dotted eighth note/sixteenth note phrases.

Several measures contain a dotted eighth note rest followed by a sixteenth note:

The 59th Street Bridge Song (Feelin' Groovy)

Words and Music by Paul Simon

62

63

64

This well-known ballad written by Charles Aznavour makes extensive use of both sixteenth and eighth note sequences throughout the song.

New chord: B♭m

She

Lyrics by Herbert Kretzmer Music by Charles Aznavour

She— may be the face I can't for-get,— a trace of plea-sure or re-
gret,— may be the trea-sure or the price I have to pay.
She— may be the song that sum-mer sings,— may be the chill that aut-umn
brings,— may be a hun-dred diff-'rent things with-in the mea-sure of a

Tunes may often go below Middle C, and others extend above top A. Further leger
lines are used for these notes.

The next two pieces have a **Coda**, an Italian word meaning 'tail'. The Coda is a separated
section of music that forms the end of an arrangement, and is represented by the
sign ⊕ .

Da Capo al Coda, usually abbreviated to **D.C. al Coda**, means return to the very
beginning (da capo) of the music, and play through again until you reach the term and
sign al Coda ⊕ just above the stave. From this point you make a skip to the Coda and
play to the end of the music.

Both tunes feature a music "punctuation" sign called the **staccato**. This is a dot placed
over (♪) or under (♩) a note, indicating that it should be shortened and detached from the
following note. Its time value remains unchanged.

Glow Worm

Traditional

Attention to correct fingering is essential in this popular classical tune. Set the Tempo at 'Medium Slow' until you can perform the cross-over fingerings smoothly.

New chord: D♭

In The Hall Of The Mountain King
(From "Peer Gynt")

By Edvard Grieg

A slur is a curved line which spans notes of differing pitch, indicating they are to be played in a smooth unbroken manner:

you   some - thing,

In songs, the lyrics often dictate where a slur is required. The syllable "some-" is a blend of two notes, to be sung *and* played smoothly.

A slur will often cover a series of notes, forming a smooth phrase:

To   Hold   Your   Hand,

I Want To Hold Your Hand" has $\mathbf{C}$ for the time signature. This denotes Common Time, and is simply another way of writing $\frac{4}{4}$ time.

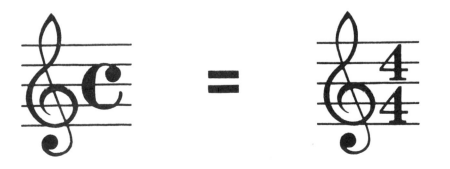

I Want To Hold Your Hand

Words and Music by John Lennon and Paul McCartney

The automatic features of the modern keyboard can be used effectively at the beginning and during the performance of a song to add variety and character.

The opening to the next song "Maria" can be played melody only, with no rhythm or chord accompaniment. Rhythm, set at 'Medium', is put on 'Key Start'. The first chord you play following the introduction will start the rhythm accompaniment.

The 'Select' button in the 'Tone Section' is a quick and easy way to change voice registration. The instrument sounds have been paired so that depressing the 'Select' button while playing gives a suitable voice contrast.

The final measure has a Fermata 𝄐 indicating that the last note can be sustained at will.

Maria
(From the Broadway Musical "West Side Story")

Music by Leonard Bernstein. Lyrics by Stephen Sondheim

76

CHANGE 'SELECT'

be!   Ma - ri - a, _____ Say   it

loud and there's mu - sic   play - ing.   Say it

soft and it's al - most like   pray - ing. _____ Ma -

ri - a, _____   I'll nev - er stop say - ing "Ma -

ri - a." _____

So far your keyboard playing has made good progress using SFX music with its letter-note identification.

'Fingered' chords have extended your playing expertise together with a working knowledge of basic harmony in left hand chord structuring.

You are now ready to play from standard music notation!

This is another major step forward that will provide new creative dimensions to keyboard playing.

Note names for the five lines and four spaces of the staff can be easily remembered by mnemonics:

Every   Good   Boy   Deserves Favours

F   A   C   E

Notes below and above the staff have the same mnemonic:

Go   Away   Big   Cat   Duck   Go   Away   Big   Cat
(below the
line!)

The waltz "Kiss Me Again" by Victor Herbert introduces standard music notation at the 16th measure.

New chord: B7

Kiss Me Again

Words and Music by Victor Herbert

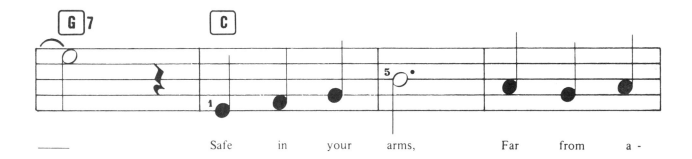

Safe   in   your   arms,   Far   from   a-

larms,   Day - light   shall   come   but   in   vain. _____

Ten - der - ly   press'd   close   to   my

breast,   Kiss   me,   Kiss   Me   A - gain. _____

"Adios Muchachos" is the ideal tune to play in Tango rhythm.

SFX letter-notes are written for the first eight measures, followed by standard music notation for the melodic repeat and finale.

Keep the tempo moderately slow to begin with, and practise up to a lively tango pace.

Adios Muchachos

Traditional

Music is often written in Cut Common Time, with the time signature:

This is $\frac{2}{2}$ time, giving a two-to-the-measure feel in the music. Instead of the quarter note representing one beat (as in Common Time, $\frac{4}{4}$), in Cut Common Time the beat becomes a half note. As a result, the music sounds twice as fast as it appears. This is simply illustrated using the lyrics and music of "Ob-La-Di, Ob-La-Da".

In Common Time, with four steady beats to the measure, the song is far too slow:

In Cut Common Time however, with two half notes to the measure and each half note having one beat

the song will flow at a much more lively pace, and the rhythm will feel right:

When playing in Cut Common Time it is best to avoid complex Rhythm and Bass accompaniments in songs with frequent chord changes.

Ob-La-Di, Ob-La-Da

Words and Music by John Lennon and Paul McCartney

84

Ob   La   Di,   Ob   La   Da,   Life   goes

on,   bra!   La   la   how   the

life   goes   on.   Ob   La

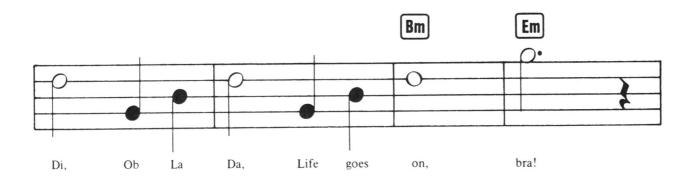

Di,   Ob   La   Da,   Life   goes   on,   bra!

La   la   how   the   life   goes   on.

Sometimes a song will have a $\frac{2}{4}$ time signature, being two quarter notes to the measure. It is a popular time signature for marches, and lively show tunes like "Diamonds Are A Girl's Best Friend".

Diamonds Are A Girl's Best Friend

Words by Leo Robin Music by Jule Styne

Key Signatures and Accidentals. A scale is a series of adjacent notes. This is the scale of C:

Only the white notes on your keyboard are used to play the scale of C.

If a scale starts on the note of F, it is necessary to play a B♭ in that scale:

As the note B♭ features throughout the scale of F, a **key signature** can be written at the beginning of the staff:

This is called the key signature of F, and it is then no longer necessary to place a flat sign before the note B in the scale:

The key signature of F indicates that every note B is flattened, irrespective of its position in or around the staff:

The song "From Me To You" is in the key of F. A number of notes in the middle section have flats written before them. These are called **accidentals**.

An accidental in a measure will apply to that particular note for the remainder of the measure:

Subsequent measures are not affected by an accidental; the notes revert back to their basic form:

keep   you   by   my   side.   I   got

Sometimes a natural sign ♮ may be used as a reminder:

keep   you   by   my   side.   I   got

A scale starting on the note G requires an F♯:

A key signature of G, with the F♯ as illustrated below, will govern that note throughout the music:

The second song "Satin Doll", is in the key of G. In the 6th measure, a natural is used to cancel the F♯. This natural is an accidental, and the key signature's F♯ again takes effect in the subsequent measures:

Out   cat - tin',   that   Sat - in   Doll._____

Remember: accidentals, whether sharps, flats, or naturals, alter the adjacent note and its recurrence within the measure only:

play - in'   it cool as can be._   give   it   a   whirl,_   but I

New chord: B♭7

From Me To You

Words and Music by John Lennon and Paul McCartney

89

New chords:

Satin Doll

Words by Billy Strayhorn and Johnny Mercer Music by Duke Ellington

91

It is often possible, and very effective, to play two or even three notes together in the right hand to enhance the melody of a song. Such supporting notes to the melody note must be carefully chosen, as they need to relate to the chord being played in your left hand.

Mrs. Robinson

Words and Music by Paul Simon

Augmented and Diminished Chords. Most keyboards are programmed for 'Fingered' chord accompaniment on the augmented and diminished chord forms.

These distinctive sounding chords are often used in popular music, and have their own symbols.

Example:

    C augmented: C aug, C+

    C diminished: C dim, C°

The chord shapes are easy to finger and learn on your keyboard.
Recurring patterns of equally spaced notes (intervals) in augmented and diminished chords result in groups of chord symbols having the same note structure:

Augmented Chords

C aug = E aug = G♯aug = A♭aug =

C♯aug = D♭aug = F aug = A aug =

D aug = F♯aug = G♭aug = A♯aug = B♭aug =

D♯aug = E♭aug = G aug = B aug =

Diminished Chords

C dim = D♯dim = E♭dim = F♯dim = G♭dim = A dim =

C♯dim = D♭dim = E dim = G dim = A♯dim = B♭dim =

D dim = F dim = G♯dim = A♭dim = B dim =

Augmented and diminished chords occasionally have numbers (5, 7,) included in the symbol. For left hand accompaniment purposes, these numbers may be disregarded; simply play the basic chord shape.